PRO BASKETBALL
★ MEGASTARS 1994 ★

Bruce Weber

SCHOLASTIC INC.

New York   Toronto   London   Auckland   Sydney

CONTENTS

Photo Credits
Cover: (Barkley, Stockton) Sports Photo Masters, Inc.; (Ewing) Allsport USA/Tim Defrisco; (Jordan) Allsport USA/Otto Greule; (Mourning) South Florida Images, Inc.; (O'Neal) South Florida Images, Inc./Richard Lewis. **4:** Focus on Sports/Peter Read. **5:** Allsport USA/Otto Greule. **6, 8, 9, 12:** Focus on Sports. **7:** South Florida Images, Inc./Al Messerschmidt. **10, 18, 19:** Sports Photo Masters, Inc./David L. Johnson. **11, 16, 17:** Sports Photo Masters, Inc. **13:** Allsport USA/Tim Defrisco. **14, 15, 27:** Sports Photo Masters, Inc./Noren Trotman. **20, 21:** Allsport USA/Tom Smart. **22:** Sportschrome, Inc./David L. Johnson. **23:** Focus on Sports/Scott Cunningham. **24:** (O'Neal) Focus on Sports/Jonathan Hayt; (Mourning) Focus on Sports/McDonough. **26:** South Florida Images, Inc. **28:** AP/Wide World. **29:** (both) AP/Wide World. **30, 31:** United Press International, Inc.

ISBN 0-590-47449-9

Copyright © 1994 by Scholastic Inc.
All rights reserved. Published by Scholastic Inc.

12 11 10 9 8 7 6 5 4 3 2 1   4 5 6 7 8 9/9

Printed in the U.S.A.
First Scholastic printing, January 1994
Book design: Doug Klein

★ PRO BASKETBALL MEGASTARS 1994: ★ WAR AND PIECE

If you watched enough NBA basketball last winter (and spring and, seemingly, early summer), you might have wondered at times what happened to the players' ice skates. Dozens of NBA players borrowed a page out of the *National Hockey League Handbook* during '92–93 and tried to settle disagreements with their fists. It wasn't enough that the league's bad actors were talking trash, now they're playing trash, too.

As a result, the NBA issued new guidelines on the eve of its '93 playoffs. Players who threw punches and missed would be suspended; players who threw punches and connected would be suspended even longer. The fines amassed in the NBA office might be enough to pay the salary of a backup guard. These days, with the average annual paycheck exceeding the million-dollar mark, a backup guard does pretty well for himself.

That's a positive step. The National Hockey League pretends it wants to end fighting which, believe it or not, isn't part of the game. The NBA is right up front in separating its game from boxing. Fight and you sit. Plain and simple. There will be fights; there will be suspensions and fines. But the league's serious stand is just what the sport needs.

Fighting aside, things couldn't be better in pro basketball. Fannies pack most of the seats all of the time and all of the seats some of the time. And those fannies buy programs and T-shirts and hot dogs and...well, you name it, so long as it has a team logo on it.

The NBA is the all-time sports marketing champ. When the NHL went searching for new leadership, it looked no farther than NBA commissioner David Stern's office. There they found top marketer Gary Bettman, whose early performance has won high marks.

Still, despite being a team sport, pro basketball's current popularity comes from its individual players. The NBA passed a major test last season when it proved it could survive nicely, thank you, without Magic Johnson and Larry Bird. That dynamic duo gets the credit for turning the world onto the NBA in the early 1980s. Now, they've gone in opposite directions. Magic wants to keep his piece of the action. He'd like to own an NBA team and, just maybe, be its coach. Larry, on the other hand, has nearly disappeared from sight—about what you'd expect.

That left Michael Jordan, who may well be the world's most recognizable athlete, to lead the parade of NBA megastars. Now he's gone, and the league will have to replace Magic, Larry, and Mike.

Perhaps the answer is Shaquille O'Neal. Reebok, for one, thinks Shaq will end up selling as many shoes as Michael has for Nike. But history says that the big guys are never the public's favorites. Over the years, players like Jerry West, Elgin Baylor, and Oscar Robertson, among others, captured the fans' undying loyalty. And those stars averaged between 6–4 and 6–7 in height. Is the world ready for a giant role model?

If Shaq makes it, then Charlotte's Alonzo Mourning will, too. Those two promise years of head-butting rammin' and jammin'. Among the current megastars, Phoenix's hugely talented Charles Barkley is the game's most fascinating character. Trouble is, his mouth often appears to run ahead of his brain. Michael Jordan has the ability to be humble; Charles Barkley simply doesn't.

The NBA, however, is blessed with its most incredible talent. Patrick Ewing has quietly become a dominant megastar. Quietly, however, is the secret word. As great as Dominique Wilkins is, he's 33. How much longer can he produce at this level? Utah's John Stockton may be the finest pure point guard ever. But he likes the public spotlight as much as he likes to get a jump shot shoved back in his face. Dennis Rodman led the league in rebounds last year, by an incredible 4.4 rebounds per game over runner-up O'Neal.

Fortunately, there are youngsters on the way. Phoenix's Cedric Ceballos was the league's top shooter in '93. Denver's Dikembe Mutombo should fit neatly into the Shaq-Mourning power pair. The Net's Kenny Anderson was well on his way to an All-Pro season last year before a freak wrist injury ended his season.

And there are more megastars on their way. Last summer's draft brought folks like Chris Webber and 7–6 Shawn Bradley and others into the league. Chances are, one or both will be on the cover of *Pro Basketball Megastars 2002!*

— *Bruce Weber*

MICHAEL JORDAN
CHICAGO BULLS

★ THE BEST EVER? ★

The final vote counts haven't arrived from Venus or Mars yet. But unless there's a nine-footer in outer space who can handle the ball like Magic Johnson, it's no contest. Michael Jordan, the best player on this planet, is probably the best player, active or retired, in the universe, too.

When *Sports Illustrated* carried an article praising Chicago Bulls' office boss Jerry Krause last spring, critics chimed in quickly. "If not for Jordan [who was there before Krause]," they all said, "the Bulls would be just another team." We like Krause, and he built a fine supporting cast around Michael, but Jordan was the engine that drove Chicago.

Michael remains the guy who drives business. According to some dollars-and-cents magazines, no. 23 is also no. 32 (in millions of dollars earned per year). Jordan is loved by fans and non-fans alike, which makes him a great salesman—for McDonald's, Nike, Gatorade, and more. Fans who tuned into Super Bowl XXVII last January expecting nothing but football were surprised. First they found Michael co-starring with Bugs Bunny in a shoe commercial. Then they saw him match Larry Bird in the weirdest game of H-O-R-S-E ever, with a Big Mac on the line. Those who sign his checks think he's worth every nickel.

Modern day basketball announcers too often refer to a great player's "athleticism." (Maybe these commentators think they get paid extra for using five-syllable words.) But athleticism's the key to Michael's on-court success. He's simply a great athlete. Even when he took batting practice with the Chicago White Sox a couple of seasons back, he swatted a couple of tape-measure homers into the upper deck in left field.

Though Michael is probably best known as a scorer (he won his record-tying seventh straight scoring title in '93 with a 32.6 ppg average), NBA insiders feared him just as much when he dished the ball to a teammate or snatched the ball from an opponent. In fact, he led the league in '93 with 2.83 steals per contest. He and teammates Scottie Pippin and Horace Grant formed a rock-solid defensive triangle that most NBA rivals found near impossible to penetrate.

There's something that simply flows whenever Jordan steps onto a basketball court—and he may well again. It's a special kind of electricity that starts with Jordan and charges up everyone who can see him.

What makes a genuine megastar? The ability to make a significant impact on a game. Michael Jordan has done exactly that. He has raised basketball to a new level and written a new standard for every player who comes along after him.

Of course, that starts with his shorts. When Michael first arrived in Chicago from the University of North Carolina, he decided he wanted ed to wear his Tarheel shorts under his Bulls' outfit. In order to do that, he ordered his pants extra-long. He started the baggy look, and now virtually every basketball player, from elementary school on up, male and female, has adopted it.

How many players in the next generation will stick out their tongues when they drive to the hoop? It will be another tribute to the man they call Air.

Even his shaved head, the result of near total baldness, has been imitated by players, even those blessed with full heads of hair. (Now, that's impact!)

But what makes Jordan the best on the planet is his zest for the game. The Knicks' Doc Rivers says, "Michael plays every play of every game like it's going to be his last." Larry Bird may have been a better long-range shooter; Oscar Robertson may have been a better rebounder as a guard; Magic Johnson was a better passer. Wilt Chamberlain might have been a better athlete. But no one ever came to play more every night and made more of his great skills than Michael.

Veteran NBA (and college) coach Larry Brown paid Michael the ultimate compliment: "I'd pay money to see him play. Heck, I'd pay money to see him *practice*!"

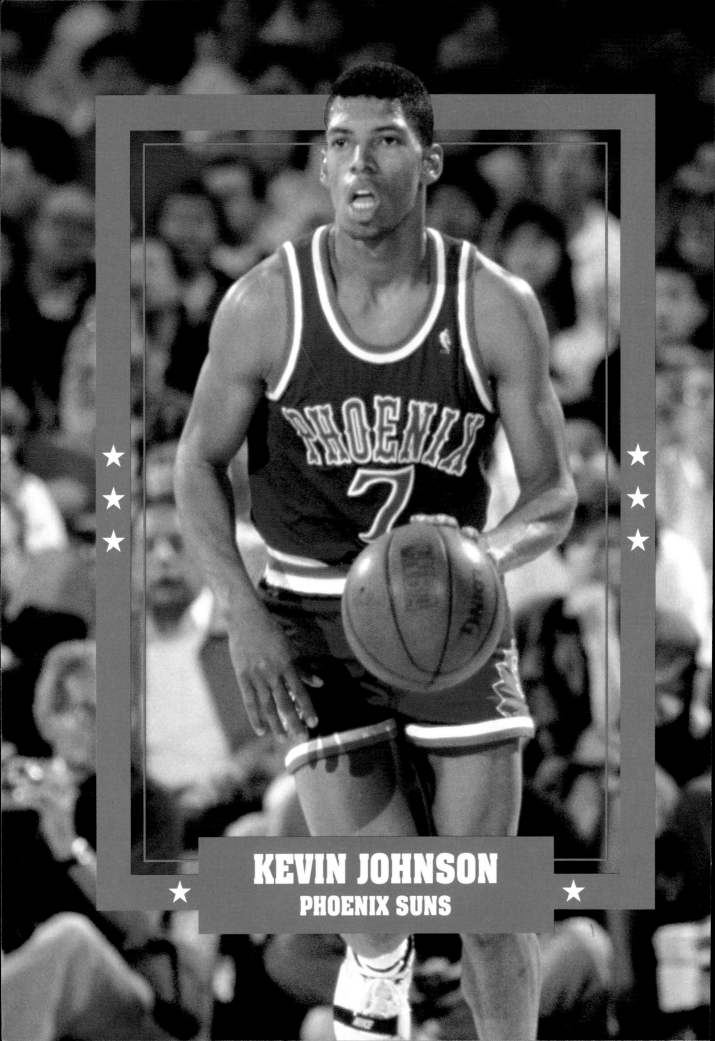

KEVIN JOHNSON
PHOENIX SUNS

★ THE DO-GOOD GUY ★

When you make a million bucks or more a year, it's easy to forget where you come from. The last thing you want to think about is your struggling youth, the grip of poverty.

Kevin Johnson of the Phoenix Suns has never forgotten. Growing up in Sacramento, California, K.J. had it as tough as anyone. But when he left, he vowed to do something great for his community. He has kept his word.

"I'm from a ghetto," says Johnson. "I can't compare it to Watts or Harlem. But Sacramento has its share of project apartment buildings. I know what the youngsters who live there are going through and I wanted to give them hope for the future."

The result? The new St. Hope Academy in Sacramento which K.J. christened during the summer of 1992. The Academy houses 10- to 16-year-old boys from the high-poverty, drug-ridden ghetto. As its name implies, St. Hope serves as a sanctuary for the youngsters and gives them a chance to take the right path socially, spiritually, culturally, and educationally.

Of course, K.J. does some of his good deeds *on* the court. His very good deeds. The three-time All-Star is always among the top guards in scoring (20 ppg) and assists (10 pg). At 6–1, he has the uncanny knack of sticking the key jumper, penetrating the stingiest defense, or hitting the open man—as the case may be.

"K.J. is one of the new breed of guards that Isiah Thomas started," says New Jersey Nets coach Chuck Daly. Daly knows what he's talking about; he coached Thomas in Detroit. "Johnson is out of the same mold, a quick, great penetrator and passer. K.J. is as good as they come."

Kevin was a first-round draft pick in 1987 after a stellar career at the University of California. On the college level, he set Cal records in scoring (1,655 points), assists (521), and steals (155). Twice he won All-Pac Ten honors.

As a pro, he spent part of his rookie season with the Cleveland Cavaliers before a blockbuster trade sent him back out west, to the Valley of the Sun. Once Johnson arrived in Phoenix, coach Cotton Fitzsimmons showed his true coaching

genius: He gave K.J. the ball and let him run the show. Blessed with a true point guard, the long-slumbering Suns were ready to shine.

The Suns won just 28 games during Kevin's first year, but then vaulted above the 50-win level in each of the next five seasons. In 1992-93, Phoenix had the league's best record and, of course, the Pacific Division and Western Conference titles. Many insiders credit the acquisition of Charles Barkley for putting the Suns over the top. But the game's *real* thinkers know that without a top-flight ball distributor like K.J., the Suns might take permanent possession of second place.

"We've tried just about everything to stop him. Nothing works," says Golden State coach Don Nelson. "Kevin is tough because he shoots so well from the outside and plays better than anyone in the open floor."

If K.J. hadn't made it in basketball, he might well have taken his great hands to the baseball diamond. In fact, he spent one summer with the Oakland Athletics' Class A team in Modesto, California. "I had to get it out of my system," says K.J. "If I hadn't, I would have wondered about it all the rest of my life."

Though Kevin has won numerous honors for his athletic accomplishments, some of his biggest awards have come off the court.

During the 1990–91 season, the Basketball Writers of America presented him with its J. Walter Kennedy Citizenship Award, named for a former NBA commissioner who also did good deeds. But perhaps the highest honor came from the White House in 1991. That's when then-President George Bush named K.J. as a "Point of Light" in his much-heralded "1000 Points of Light."

K.J. has earned it all!

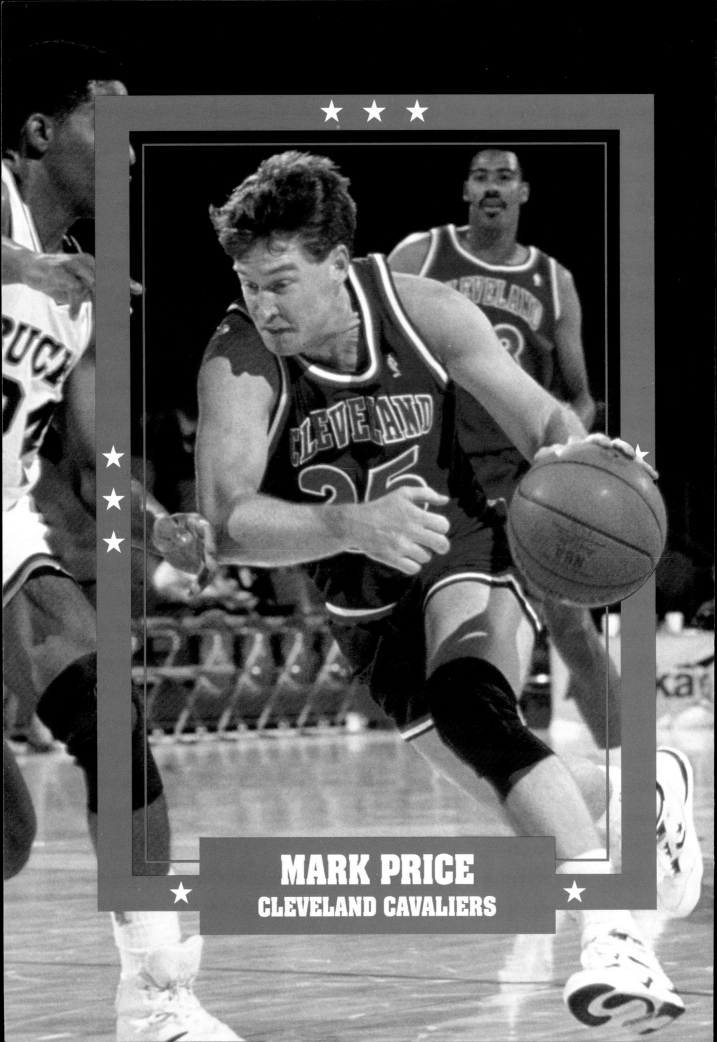

MARK PRICE
CLEVELAND CAVALIERS

★ THE BULL'S-EYE MAN ★

Cleveland's Mark Price is the kind of guy who needs to convince the gate guard at NBA arenas that he's one of the visiting players. He isn't very big; he isn't very powerful. But with a basketball in his hands, he's absolutely frightening.

Folks around the NBA have always known about the great things Mark can do for a ball club. But it took a spectacular 1993 All-Star Weekend to show casual observers. On Saturday, he unseated two-time champion Craig Hodges in the Long Distance Shootout. His pinpoint accuracy earned him a hard-fought 18–17 victory over Portland's Terry Porter.

"I went first," remembers Price, "and I was really relaxed. I had nothing to lose. I didn't expect to win—and I wasn't alone." When Porter stepped behind the arc, he was on fire. He cut the gap to one point with five shots still left. "I thought he had it," said Price. But Terry misfired down the stretch and handed the title to Mark.

The following day, in the All-Star Game, Price tossed in 19 points and delivered four assists in only 23 minutes for the East squad. National TV audiences were impressed.

If you like the way Mark shoots threes, you've got to love him at the foul line. Going into the '93 season, he was hitting free throws at 89.9%, just one-tenth of one percent behind career leader Rick Barry's 90%. And he hits them in clumps, with streaks of 51, 45, 42, and 40 during the '92 campaign. In '93, he led the league by hitting 94.8% from the charity stripe. Bottom line: When the game is on the line and the Cavs need a bucket, they know who can stick it in the hole for them.

He doesn't do it alone, of course. Cleveland is at its best when Price is drilling from outside and dishing off to the big guys, Brad Daugherty and Larry Nance, inside. When the trio is on, the Cavs can play with anyone. In the '92 playoffs, when Chicago expected to romp through the east on the way to a second straight title, Cleveland made it very tough in the conference finals. They took the Bulls to six games, with Price averaging 19 points and seven assists per game. He also shot better than 90% from the line and had a high-game performance of 35.

It was Cleveland's first-ever trip to the conference finals. They had already beaten New Jersey and Boston after a franchise-record 57 regular-season wins.

Though the Cavs came up a buck short, Price had to be satisfied with his—and the team's—performance. The previous season (1990–91) had been a classic bummer. On November 30, 1990, just 16 games into the season, Mark blew out the anterior cruciate ligament in his knee and missed the rest of the season. At the time, Mark was leading the league in free-throw percentage (95.2%) and was among the elite in assists and steals. His injury set the tone for the season. The Cavs were hit hard by the injury bug and wound up losing to Philadelphia in the opening round of the playoffs. That's why Mark's comeback season was so rewarding.

Though Price has been an NBA leader practically from day one, it didn't come as much of a surprise to basketball insiders. Mark comes from a great basketball family. His father, Denny, is the athletic director and former head basketball coach at Phillips University in Oklahoma. He has also spent time as an NBA assistant coach.

Mark's brother Brent enjoyed an outstanding career as a sharpshooting guard (what else?) at the University of Oklahoma and was a first-round selection by his current employers, the Washington Bullets, in the NBA draft.

That's typical of the Prices. Mark had been a key man in a major turnaround at his alma mater, Georgia Tech. Long an ACC doormat (they were 4–23 the year before he arrived), Price and current Miami Heat star John Salley led the way for Bobby Cremins' Yellow Jackets. Mark became the first freshman in ACC history to lead the league in scoring. As a junior, he and Salley led Tech to the Eastern Regional finals before they fell to Patrick Ewing's super-talented Georgetown squad. That's Mark Price: winner!

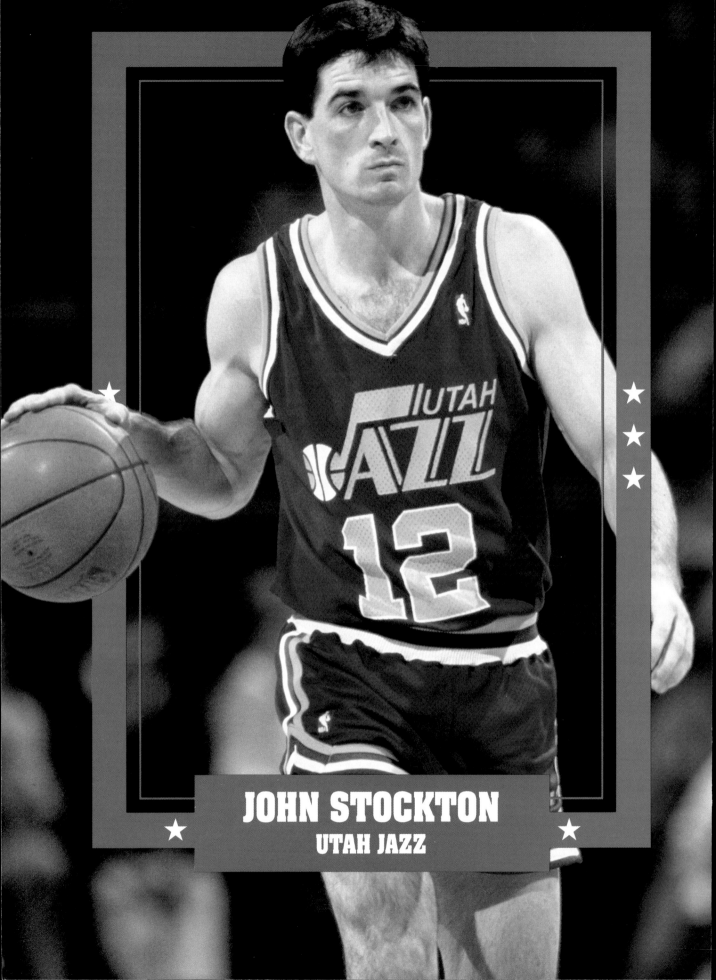

JOHN STOCKTON
UTAH JAZZ

n the NBA dictionary, under the term *point guard*, there's a picture of John Stockton. Okay, old joke. But there should be. Stockton, a total unknown when he came to the Jazz out of Gonzaga University in Spokane, Washington, has defined the position like no other point guard in decades. A complete ball-handler, passer, and team leader, he sets the standard for every other point guard in the league.

It's tough to pinpoint Stockton's greatest skill. Perhaps it's enough to say that he just runs the show. Teamed with Karl Malone, one of the NBA's leading power forwards, he gives the Jazz an outstanding Mr. Inside-Mr. Outside combo.

More than a few eyebrows were raised (notably in Detroit) when Stockton was chosen as the U.S. Olympic Dream Team point guard over the Pistons Isiah Thomas. But there were few doubters in the Dreamers training camp. Everyone in the league knows exactly what John Stockton can do for a team.

How unknown was Stockton when the Jazz made him the 16th pick in the first round of the 1984 NBA draft? "Some of our fans were angry and confused," remembers director of basketball operations, Scott Layden. "I guess they thought we'd picked Dick Stockton of CBS-TV."

It was no mistake. By the time he's finished, Stockton will rank among the league's all-timers at point guard. Only Magic Johnson, Oscar Robertson, and Thomas rank ahead of him on the career-assist list.

John is extremely popular with Jazz fans. He's always available for public appearances, and the press gets access to him whenever it needs to. Stockton is equally happy with Salt Lake City. "It's a lot like Spokane," he says, referring to his hometown. In fact, John splits his year between his two hometowns, living in a home next door to his parents during the off-season.

While many NBA players would love to get the attention Michael Jordan got, Stockton avoids the spotlight. "I had a traditional middle-class upbringing," he says, "and that includes a need for privacy."

NBA watchers are convinced that Stockton would be heavily pursued for commercials and endorsements if he played in one of the league's bigger cities, like New York or Chicago or Los Angeles. Asked if he'd like that scenario, Stockton answers simply, "No, no, a thousand times no." Bottom line: Even though John wears and endorses Nike footwear, there will never be a line of Air Stockton shoes.

Being an unknown has never hurt John's career. He wound up at Gonzaga U. after four years at Gonzaga Prep, just down the street. Spokane wasn't on anyone's recruiting map and John took whatever he could.

Gonzaga turned out to be a fine choice. His father and grandfather both starred there. Some still regard his grandfather, Houston Stockton, as the greatest football player in Gonzaga history. (The football program was dropped years ago.)

Even though he enjoyed a superb college career, it wasn't until it was almost over that he thought he'd even get a chance to prove himself in the NBA. "I always felt I could compete," he says. "I just wanted the opportunity. I've always enjoyed basketball; starring in the NBA was just the gravy."

It's significant that Stockton plays for a team whose nickname involves music. His activities on the court remind some experts of an orchestra conductor. "He's the maestro," says longtime rival Fat Lever. "It's like having an extra coach out there when John is running the offense. He doesn't make a lot of mistakes and he always controls the ball. When it gets down to gut-check time, he's going to be in charge. He demands respect out there and he gets it because his team-mates know that he knows what he's doing."

PATRICK EWING
NEW YORK KNICKS

★ THE NEXT MAYOR OF NEW YORK? ★

Ever since that spring day in 1985, Patrick Ewing has been a marked man. When NBA Commissioner David Stern picked the Knicks card for the top choice in the first-ever draft lottery, New York general manager Dave DeBusschere raised his arms in triumph. Ewing, Georgetown's super big man, would be a Knick.

Victory-starved New York fans were convinced that the native of Jamaica would hang countless NBA championship banners from the ceiling of the big round building on the city's west side. If ever a rookie came to a ballclub with pressure squarely on his back, it was Ewing.

Problem was that nobody bothered to ask the rest of the Knicks if they were up to winning a championship. No one wins a basketball title by himself. As big and as talented as Patrick Ewing is, he couldn't do it alone. And the Knicks simply didn't have the talent to support their superstar.

And that's exactly what Ewing has become. By the time the '93 season ended, everyone was about ready to concede that Patrick was the best center in the league. By sheer hard work, the seven-footer had overcome virtually all of his weaknesses. Always a fine outside shooter, he had polished his inside game so that he was a threat every time he touched the ball. Although he doesn't have the best pair of hands in the league, he had become a fierce rebounder. Once the Knicks managed to provide the kind of support Patrick needed up front (Charles Smith, Charles Oakley, and Anthony Mason), the big guy could do his thing. When he got the ball down low, he could power up, dribble across the lane for a pull-up jumper, or back out for his unstoppable fade-away "J."

Through the years, as the Knicks continued to struggle despite having Ewing in the pivot, fans around the league jumped all over Patrick. He was, they believed, an underachiever. That simply isn't true.

Ewing has always been a winner. At Cambridge Rindge & Latin High School in Massachusetts, he went from gawky to great, leading his school to three straight state titles. At Georgetown, he took the Hoyas to three NCAA finals in four years, including a championship in 1984. Already a fine scorer, he became a huge force on defense in college. And he was part of the U.S. Olympic gold medal team in 1984—with Michael Jordan, Chris Mullin, and Sam Perkins, among others. There simply isn't a tougher competitor than the Knicks' big man.

But things weren't easy in New York. In addition to overly high expectations, the Knicks were frequently confused. First came the experiment that sent Patrick to forward with Bill Cartwright at center. That didn't work. The Knicks played "musical coaches," switching from Hubie Brown to Bob Hill to Rick Pitino. And just when it looked like Ewing's longtime friend Pitino would make things happen, the coach took off for the University of Kentucky. Then came more coaching changes, from Stu Jackson to John MacLeod. Patrick was scoring and rebounding, but the team was going nowhere.

The move that got things going for Patrick and the ballclub was the arrival of coach Pat Riley in 1991. It came at about the same time Ewing had asked to be traded in a contract dispute. The Knicks won an arbitration case that kept the big man in the Big Apple. And things took off from there.

Riley got everyone playing defense like Ewing played defense. Some fans—and some players, in fact—thought the Knicks had become a "dirty" team. But Patrick and his mates knew that they were just playing aggressively within the rules. With Riley and the new Knicks on board, Patrick became a scoring machine (24.2 ppg in '93, sixth in the league). More important, his rebounding (12.1 pg last year) and his presence down low in the paint opened up the outside scoring game for John Starks and Doc Rivers, among others.

There was a time, a couple of decades ago, when a Knick team of future Hall of Famers like Bill Bradley, Walt Frazier, and Willis Reed owned the big town. Now, with Patrick Ewing at the top of his game and the rest of the Knicks playing like champions most nights, a ticket to a Knicks game is the toughest ticket in town. And Patrick Ewing, as the story goes, could be elected mayor, if he really wanted the job.

DAVID ROBINSON
SAN ANTONIO SPURS

★ THE ADMIRABLE ADMIRAL ★

Basketball coaches at the United States Naval Academy recruit with at least one arm tied behind their backs. Problem is the Academy's height limit. No plebe (freshman) may stand taller than 6–8. Their opponents work with no such limit. The result is that Navy teams are often undersized—and overmatched.

That's part of the miracle of David Robinson. The San Antonio Spurs' 7–1 megastar center, a featured player on the U. S. Olympic Dream Team, is a Navy graduate, the only midshipman on any pro basketball roster. How did that happen?

When David came to the Annapolis, Maryland, institution in 1983, he had only one year of basketball experience and was only 6–7, one inch under the USNA limit. He also came in with a 1320 score on the SAT test. No, Robinson was unlike most college hoopsters—and *then* he became a great one!

Early on, David was just a scholar. He was fascinated by science, loved music, and was consumed by reading just about anything. Sports was way down on his list of interests. He even quit his first high school team because he didn't think he'd play much. How was his coach to know that this 5–5 runt was going to grow up into an NBA superstar center?

David was 6–6 as a high school senior at Osbourn Park High in northern Virginia. The basketball coach practically drafted Robinson onto the basketball team, hoping the youngster would like the game. Though David would have preferred gymnastics, he gave his new sport his best shot.

The rest is history. In his first year at Navy, Robinson broke his hand boxing. The doctor told coach Paul Evans that this kid was going to grow some more. And did he ever! Navy's first and only seven-footer became the first college player to amass more than 2,500 points, 1,300 rebounds, and a 60%+ shooting percentage. He led Navy to 60 wins in 70 games his last two years. And he was a prime NBA pick in the 1987 draft.

But there was that small matter of service in the Navy. The Spurs picked him knowing that he wouldn't be available for at least a season or two. Meanwhile, the best players in the NBA were earning more in one half of a game than David was making in a whole month in the Navy.

But it was worth the wait. By the time this giant David met the other Goliaths of the NBA, he was ready. He tossed in 24.3 points per game, blocked 3.9 shots, and grabbed 12 rebounds. How important was Robinson to the Spurs? The year before he arrived, San Antonio had gone 21–61, bottom-of-the-barrel numbers. With Robby occupying the middle, they went 56–26, an incredible 35-game turnaround. His Rookie of the Year award surprised exactly no one.

And it hasn't stopped there. Robinson, like so many great big men, makes San Antonio a threat to win every night. Although the Spurs couldn't overcome an early-season slump (under short-lived coach Jerry Tarkanian) and a late-season sag in '93, David helped lead the undermanned Spurs to second place in the Midwest Division with his 23.4 points per game scoring, his 11.7 rebounds per game, and his 3.22 blocks per outing.

"I got a late start," Robinson says. "I didn't play high scool ball 'til my last year and didn't get serious about the game until my sophomore year of college. But when I get serious about something, I give it one hundred percent. I can't live with myself unless I try to be the best I can be."

In his relatively short pro career, Robinson has made lots of fans. Count his old coach Larry Brown among them. "Rarely have I seen such grace, speed, and quickness in a seven-foot, one-inch player."

Of course, David's devotion to academics hasn't been lost in the battle that is the NBA. "Education is very important to me," he says. He donates considerable time and money to various organizations that help young children. In fact, a couple of years ago, he adopted a fifth-grade class at a San Antonio elementary scool. Each student will earn $2,300 from a special fund if—and when—he or she graduates from high school. That's the kind of man David Robinson is—and the kind of legacy he wants to leave.

CHARLES BARKLEY
PHOENIX SUNS

★ THE MOUTH THAT ROARED ★

When the Philadelphia 76ers traded Sir Charles Barkley to the Phoenix Suns before the 1992–93 season, there was rejoicing in some parts of Philly and dread in certain quarters of Arizona. There was no question that the so-called Round Mound of Rebound was a genuine talent, a man who could bring an entire team to a higher level.

But there was also that "mouth" thing. Charles Barkley is the most outspoken player in the NBA—and he has an opinion on everything. When his autobiography appeared in bookstores everywhere, there were some unkind remarks about several of his Sixer teammates. No problem: "I was misquoted," said Barkley. Huh?

Last January, displeased with a couple of calls in a Phoenix game at New York, Barkley decided to "discuss" matters with an official. At the end of the game, he vaulted over the scorer's table, accidently pulling the plug on the building's computer system. When the official threatened to ask for a huge fine against the superstar, Barkley shouted, "You can't control me with money." His outburst cost him about $40,000, but when you're making about four million a year, who cares about 40 grand. Certainly not Charles Barkley.

It's not just his mouth that's big. Everything about him is, except for his height. Once reported to be 6–7, Charles measures out at about 6–4, tiny by NBA standards for power forwards. At about 252 pounds, however, Barkley is like a runaway truck on the court. No one who values his life gets in his way when he rolls (literally) to the basket. As a result, he is a 25 ppg scorer. And he's the supreme go-to guy. When the game is on the line, it's Sir Charles who wants the ball. In that game in New York, Barkley's discussion with the referee immediately followed an ill-advised three-point attempt that could have won the game for Phoenix.

That, of course, is what Barkley does best. The Suns were not only willing to let Charles run off at the mouth, they were willing to let him lead their team. Long a second-banana in the Pacific Division (usually behind the L.A. Lakers), Phoenix zoomed to the league's best record after Barkley arrived last season.

"The trade from Philadelphia turned my career around," said Barkley. "All of a sudden, I was free." It changed Charles' address but not his attitude.

"I'm the best," he says. "I'm the Ninth Wonder of the World." And he has the numbers to back up that blather. He also has his share of special admirers.

"His body build, his great skill, and his incredible quickness make him the most unique player I've ever seen," says L.A. Laker Hall of Famer and office boss Jerry West. He also owns the best first step in the game and some of the trickiest moves ever seen on a basketball court.

Charles always plays the game like a man on a mission. Usually, that's exactly the case.

Overlooked by most recruiters in high school (he was 6–2 and weighed about 260), he put away the state's best in a late-season head-to-head battle. Given a shot at Auburn University, he became an All-SEC sensation by shooting 63.6% for his college career. He also led the loop in rebounding in each of his three seasons. Not bad for a 6–4 forward carrying nearly 290 pounds on his frame.

Cut by the U.S. Olympic coaching staff in 1984, he vowed to get even some day. He did it in '92, leading the Dream Team in its gold medal victories.

Drafted by the Sixers as the fifth choice of the first round, Philly quickly found a starting spot for the newcomer and let him learn the game from his teammates, Julius Erving and Moses Malone. "That was great," remembers Barkley. "Julius took care of the scoring and Moses took care of the rebounding. And I just picked up the tricks of the trade."

About the only thing he didn't accomplish in Philly was winning a championship banner for the rafters. It's something that the new America West Arena in Phoenix could use.

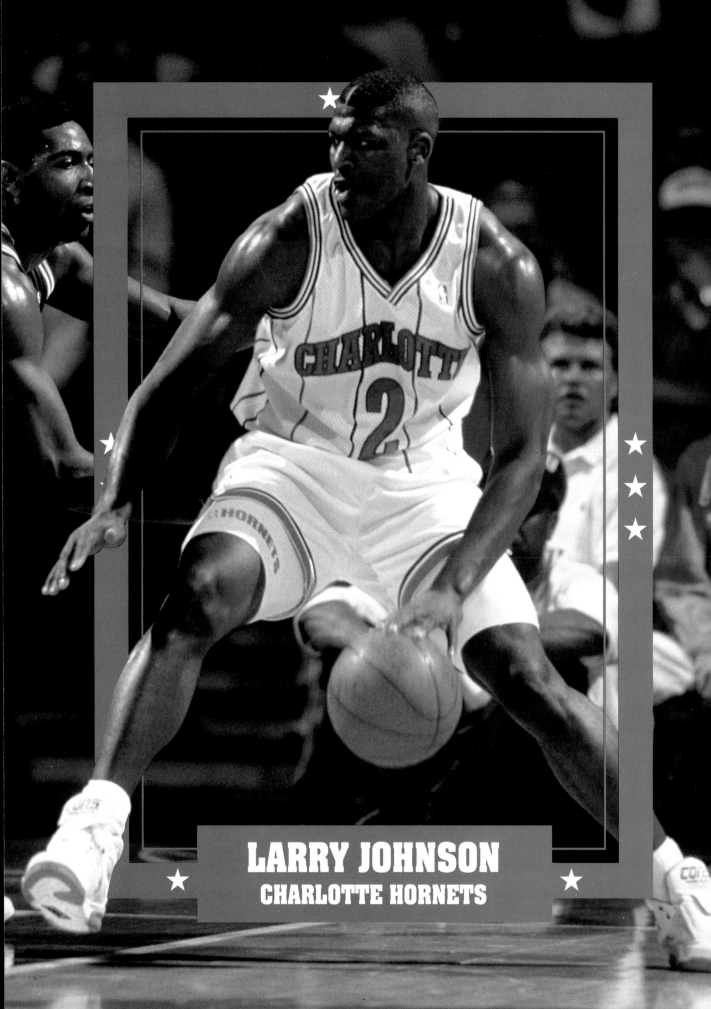

LARRY JOHNSON
CHARLOTTE HORNETS

Boston fans are going to holler, but there's a new "Larry Legend" on the horizon. And he doesn't wear Celtic green.

It's Larry Johnson of the Charlotte Hornets and, with teammate Alonzo Mourning, he could make Hornet-teal-and-blue the NBA colors of the next decade.

Johnson has a way to go before replacing Larry Bird on the league's all-time lists, but he's taken the first few giant steps. Actually, Johnson has been a legend for some time, starting on the playgrounds on the tough south side of Dallas, his hometown.

It seems that the term "man-child" was created especially for Larry. Even as a young teenager, he was a child in a man's body. But he certainly didn't play basketball like a child. To go with his size, he also owned the moves of a whirling dervish, the power of a Greek god, and the gold-toothed grin of another Johnson of long ago, the Bullets' Gus Johnson.

Everyone around Green Bay Park in Dallas knew Larry. His boisterous laugh could be heard ringing throughout the park. And he worked. Did he always work? His mom says she never worried about Larry. The neighborhood may have been overrun with crime and violence and drugs. But Larry's mom always knew where her "little boy" was—at the park, working on his game. "Even when it got late," said mom Dortha, "I just looked out the window and there he was!"

After an all-everything career at Dallas' Skyline High (some experts think he was the best high school player in America as a senior), Larry decided he wasn't ready for college. Fact is, his grades didn't qualify him for most four-year schools. So off he went to Odessa (Texas) Junior College where he was the national junior college Player of the Year—twice! Finally, he was ready.

Nevada-Las Vegas coach Jerry Tarkanian had been keeping his eye on Johnson and, when the time came, the Shark welcomed the new legend with open arms. Johnson led the Runnin' Rebels to an NCAA title and his four years at Odessa and Las Vegas produced an incredible 134–13 record!

Now, Larry's playground is the Charlotte Coliseum, where 23,000 paying customers have replaced the Johnson fan club in Green Bay Park. The Hornets aren't there yet, but there's a strong likelihood that they'll be among the league's best teams within the next season or two. And when they get there, Johnson should be right out in front.

There was one obstacle for Johnson to conquer before he became an NBA megastar. It's the one that no amount of practice can help: height. At UNLV, Johnson was listed at 6–7. But when he arrived at Charlotte, with considerable fanfare, the tape-measure stretched to only a shade over 6–5. Had he shrunk? Not really. His was just another case of college teams exaggerating their players' sizes. No matter. Blessed with an immovable 250-pound frame and the reach of a player far taller, Johnson could more than hold his own, posting up in the paint.

That's not the only posting he did. With rookie numbers including 19 points and 11 rebounds, a pair of 34-point games, and double-figure scoring in 77 of his 82 contests, he was a shoo-in for Rookie of the Year honors. By the '93 season, his second, his scoring was up to 22.1 ppg, 12th in the NBA. He also averaged 10.5 rebounds per contest.

"Larry simply doesn't have any weaknesses," boasts Hornet coach Allen Bristow. "I've been around a lot of great players in this league, but all of them had soft spots in their game. Not Larry."

Although the Hornets made him the league's number-one draft choice in 1991, they could be accused of overconfidence. They had to win the draft lottery before they could claim the '91 Wooden Award (college MVP) winner. But Charlotte management was so certain they'd win, they printed up a jersey with his name and favorite uniform number (no. 2) before draft day.

That's confidence. That's what makes Larry Johnson a winner and what will make the Charlotte Hornets winners, too.

KARL MALONE
UTAH JAZZ

★ NO POSTAGE DUE ★

Just about the best thing that ever happened to Karl Malone was an accident of scheduling. The NBA likes to put its All-Star Weekend festival into its newest arenas. So when the Utah Jazz opened up shop at The Delta Center in Salt Lake City, commissioner David Stern & "Partners" slotted the 1993 game there. It was exactly what "The Mailman" ordered.

Blessed with just about the best body in the NBA, Karl Malone has also been one of the league's best kept secrets. Oh, sure, everybody knew about the big guy. After all, he was a member of the fabled U.S. Olympic Dream Team. But because of the Jazz's relatively low profile and Mountain-Time-zone home, few basketball nuts got to see him enough to *really* know him.

That's why the All-Star Game, with its high ratings and national TV audience, was perfect. Given the opportunity, Karl really responded. In leading the West to a 135–132 victory ("Can you say DEFENSE?," Mr. Rogers asked his neighborhood.), Malone poured in 28 points and grabbed 10 rebounds in 34 minutes. He delighted the hometown crowd, wowed the millions watching on the tube, and impressed the media, which voted him co-MVP with fellow-Jazz John Stockton.

It figured that Malone would wind up playing in Utah. His basketball career has always taken him just slightly off the beaten track. He played high school basketball in Summerfield, Louisiana, not exactly a high school hoops hotbed. That means the major college scouts didn't see him, and the major schools didn't offer him a scholarship.

So Karl wound up at Louisiana Tech, another non-hotbed, in Ruston, Louisiana, where he had to sit out his freshman year because of poor high school grades. From then on, however, it was up, up, and away for the budding Superman.

By his junior year (after failing to make the 1984 U.S. Olympic Team), he led Tech to its first-ever Top Ten rating and the finals of the NCAA Midwest Regional in Dallas. His career numbers of 18.7 points and 56.6% shooting made him a marked man.

So when he decided to leave Tech for the NBA, he was a hot item. The Jazz picked him

early, confident that they owned a franchise player. And they did—except for the stripe in the round circle 15 feet from the basket. Malone scored 14.9 ppg and grabbed 718 rebounds while averaging 32 minutes per game. But free throws were another story. Malone missed more than he made, a major concern for anyone who went to the line as often as he did.

The solution? Same as any for Karl: hard work and long hours. These days he flirts with the 80% mark on foul shots, far above the league average.

Though Malone's well-sculpted body earns respect from opponents and admiration from fans, it's a subject Malone dislikes discussing. "I don't

work out for glory," he says. "I do it because it's necessary. My strength and endurance give me and my team an advantage. I want to keep that advantage."

Playing on the Dream Team in the summer of '92 was a career highlight for Malone. Although it seemed he'd never get a shot at the Olympics after being cut in '84, it was always a dream of his. "I was so let down back then. I tried out for a month and then was dismissed. I was determined someday to prove those coaches wrong."

Thus his selection in '92 was especially meaningful, especially because that team set the standards by which all future teams will be judged.

Was it worth giving up his off-season to go to Barcelona? "You've got that right," said Malone. "It was a thrill for me to compete for my country and, of course, to win a gold medal. The entire experience was amazing. The players, the coaches, and the fans made it something I will never forget."

Meanwhile, back in Utah, the higher-profile Malone sets his sights on what most outsiders would consider the really impossible dream: turning Utah into hoop heaven.

DOMINIQUE WILKINS
ATLANTA HAWKS

When the 1992–93 season started, everyone in Atlanta held their collective breath. Dominique Wilkins, long the Hawks' leader, was coming off surgery for a ruptured Achilles tendon, an injury that has ended many NBA careers. And when the victim is 33 years old with 10 pro seasons behind him, it's twice as tough to come back.

On the Hawks opening weekend, 'Nique played 75 minutes, scored 63 points, and sank 52% of his shots. The sound of breath being exhaled in Atlanta could be heard all the way to Birmingham.

Wilkins has long been Georgia's favorite son. A superstar at the University of Georgia before suiting up for Atlanta, he has long carried his special nickname (The Human Highlight Film) with great pride. A two-time All-American at Georgia, Dominique averaged 22 points and seven rebounds per game for the Bulldogs, leading the team to a rare post-season tournament.

Entering the NBA draft after his junior year, Wilkins was selected by the Utah Jazz (as the third pick of the first round). But 'Nique never played a minute in Salt Lake City. The Jazz dealt him back home (for a couple of players who'd outlived their usefulness). It's one trade the Jazz would love to forget.

Even before the injury that ended his '92 season, Dominique was already playing under enormous pressure. Hawks fans were hugely disappointed when Wilkins was left off the roster of the Olympic Dream Team. And 'Nique himself was upset that so many of his best friends had been dealt off the Atlanta roster. Still, the man has enormous pride, which drove him to a full, maybe better-than-ever, recovery.

"Everybody had this wait-and-see attitude," he says. "But when I got off to such a great start, I answered all of the questions. That opening weekend was so important. I think a lot of folks saw enough to know instantly that I was back. I knew I could do it."

Wilkins actually attributes the Achilles tendon injury to his fast start in '92–93. "Before I got hurt, I used to treat the off-season as a vacation. Why not? After 82 games plus playoffs, after hanging out in too many airports to count, I would simply kick back until training camp. While I was in

rehab, I certainly couldn't do that."

Around the Hawks' camp, Dominique had earned a reputation as a slow starter. He always played himself into shape. Now that's all changed.

"I'm not getting any younger," 'Nique says. "I finally learned that I had to take care of myself during the off-season."

Before and after the injury, Wilkins was on top of his game. Before the injury, Dominique was *magnifique* (that's French for magnificent). The French-born (his dad was in the army) forward put up huge pre-'93 numbers—26.2 points, seven rebounds, 2.6 assists, 80.9% from the line, and

47% from the field—all of which demonstrated 'Nique's dominance in a league of superstars. After the injury, he was perhaps more effective. When he spun and drove from the left side against Seattle last winter, he scored his 20,885th point, setting an all-time Hawks' franchise record. The basket accounted for two of Wilkins' 34 points that night (a 118-109 Atlanta victory).

Even though 'Nique came back in the best shape of his life, the season wasn't all fun and games. He was averaging 27.7 points per game when a broken right hand sidelined him for a month (until mid-January). Even then, the new-attitude Wilkins came shining through. Atlanta doctors predicted Dominique would be out for six to eight weeks with the hand injury. He was back in four. At season's end, he had canned 29.9 ppg, second only to Michael Jordan.

"People questioned 'Nique's commitment," says Knicks' guard Doc Rivers, a long-time Hawk teammate of Wilkins. "They said he couldn't come back to what he was. But I know Dominique better than that. He's a competitor through and through. When he heard—and I knew he would—that people were doubting his ability to return at full strength, he responded big time."

There's no question about it. Dominique *is magnifique*!

SHAQUILLE O'NEAL
ORLANDO MAGIC

ALONZO MOURNING
CHARLOTTE HORNETS

★ WAR ON THE BOARDS ★

t's almost an unbreakable law of sports. *Nobody* roots for Goliath. When the New York Yankees were dominating baseball during the 1950s, Yankee haters clearly outnumbered Yankee lovers. When Wilt Chamberlain was tossing in 50 points a game, lots of fans had no use for the giant from Philly. It has always been like that.

Until now. With Larry Bird, Magic Johnson, and Michael Jordan retired, the guard (and the center) will be changing in the NBA. And the new heroes may well be those gigantic wonders, Shaquille "The Real Deal" O'Neal and Alonzo Mourning.

There's something so genuinely likeable about Shaq (pronounced *shack*) that the "hate the giant" law may have to be repealed. That he's talented is not in question. He's one of those rare types who can take over a game all by himself. He moves like a man a half-foot smaller. He occupies an incredible amount of space under the basket. He's tough enough to handle any kind of physical challenge thrown up by an opponent. And can handle the off-court pressures just as easily.

In short, the seven-foot, 300-pounder from LSU, the first $40-million man in sports (on a seven-year contract), may be the player of the nineties—and the twenty-first century, too! Certainly the folks at Reebok think O'Neal's the guy. They're paying him Michael-Jordan-type money to sell their shoes like Mike has for Nike. But if Michael co-stars with Bugs Bunny in his commercials, who can match up with Shaq? Disney's Beast?

Meanwhile, Shaq did his 1993 talking on the court. Although Orlando barely missed the play-offs, they couldn't blame it on the man-child O'Neal. In his rookie season, he averaged 23.4 points per game. He also hit 56.2% from the field and trailed only San Antonio's Dennis Rodman in the rebounding battle with 13.9 per outing. He also blocked 3.53 shots per game, again good for second in the league.

Meanwhile, up in Charlotte, one-time Georgetown ace Mourning was busy putting the Hornets right into the thick of the playoff hunt. A one-time Gatorade National High School Player of the Year, Mourning didn't really demonstrate his power at Georgetown until his senior year when

twin tower Dikembe Mutombo had graduated to the NBA.

Joining 1992 rookie of the year Larry Johnson at Charlotte, Alonzo instantly won the confidence of his teammates and coach Alan Bristow. He wound up with a solid 21.0 ppg scoring average (15th in the league and trailing Johnson's 22.1 on the Hornets). He also grabbed 10.5 rebounds and blocked 3.47 shots per game. Charlotte's front line became one of the league's most feared, a major turnaround in a two-year period.

For both O'Neal and Mourning, match-ups with New York's Patrick Ewing were season highlights. For O'Neal, it was a chance to go head-to-head with the player considered the league's best at his position. Ewing was coming off his Dream Team summer, and the Knicks were romping toward the best record in the NBA East. When Shaq keyed a last-minute 10-point comeback for an Orlando home victory in early March, he convinced everyone that he was, indeed, "The Real Deal."

It was a little different for Mourning, who had matched body slams with the Knicks' star throughout his college career. Ewing, who preceded (and helped recruit) Mourning at Georgetown, had spent his off-seasons working with the youngster. Everytime they met in the 1992–93 season, it was a take-no-prisoners pitched battle—among friends.

Both of the big guys will be around for awhile. Shaq got a seven-year, $40-million deal to sign with Orlando. Mourning had to settle for a slightly lower tax bracket. Neither will ever be poor again. But for NBA watchers who are looking for the match-up of this—and the next—century, it's Shaq vs. Alonzo. Take that to the bank!

COACH PAT RILEY
NEW YORK KNICKS

★ HUDSON RIVER SHOWDOWN ★

f the folks at NBA Entertainment ever decide to produce a soap opera, they've got all the makings right in their own backyard. Within a five-mile radius of their Secaucus, New Jersey, studios, the principal gunfighters are all dressed up (*really* dressed up) and ready to go. It's time for *Gunfight at the NBA Corral*, starring the old bushwhacker Pat Riley and pistol-packin' Chuck Daly. If ever two gunslingers were ready to battle for turf, it's the coaches of the New York Knicks and New Jersey Nets.

Unlike most western horse operas, there's no guy in the white hat. These fellas don't wear hats. But the rest of their outfits are right out of the latest fashion magazines. Riley, who spends more on haircuts than most guys do on suits, is younger and slicker. Daly, whose clothes closet may be big enough to scrimmage in, is a little older, maybe a little wiser, and tough as nails.

The folks at Madison Square Garden fired the first shot in the Hudson River War when they

hired Riley away from NBC-TV following the 1990–91 season. Riley brought excellent credentials to the job, despite losing his final half-time in-studio shooting contest to pint-sized Bob Costas. Before that, Riley had enjoyed a decent playing career with the Lakers and then led the team to four NBA titles in nine years. One came at the expense of Daly's Detroit Pistons. Perhaps most important, Pat had managed to blend a cast of great individual talents into one of the most entertaining teams ever seen.

The Knick's needed him. They needed him badly. The once-proud New York franchise had crumbled, slipping to the NBA depths following its only two league championships in 1970 and 1973. Even famous savior Hubie Brown had failed to stop the bleeding. Knick fans who thought that Patrick Ewing would bring them title after title when he was selected as the league's top draft pick in 1985 were hugely disappointed. So it was Riley to the rescue—and just in the *knick* of time!

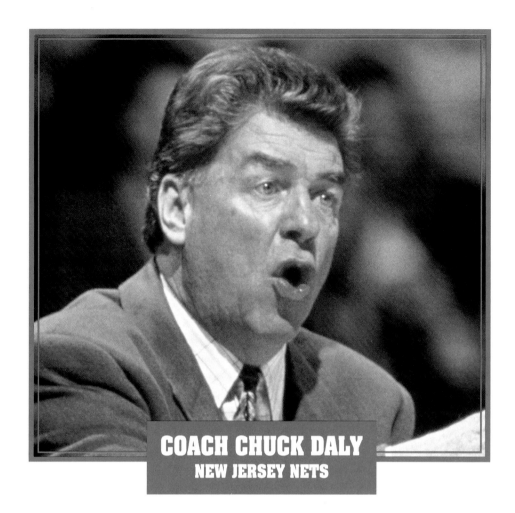

COACH CHUCK DALY
NEW JERSEY NETS

Meanwhile, over in the Jersey Meadowlands, the Nets' proudest moments had come in a different state and in a different league. Led by Julius Erving and Rick Barry, the New York Nets had been a dominant team in the old American Basketball Association and promised to play a major role in the NBA when the two leagues merged. It wasn't to be. The Nets didn't have enough money to keep Erving, who was shipped to Philadelphia. With him went the last blessed memories of the powerful Nets, who later moved to New Jersey.

Enter the new gun in town, Chuck Daly. At age 62, the dapper Daly was fresh off a sweeping, though not unexpected, victory with the Dream Team in Barcelona. Not incidently, he owned two NBA championship rings, courtesy of his former team, the Detroit Pistons. In fact, one of the squad's back-to-back titles was won at the expense of Riley and his Lakers.

The stage was set. Practically cast aside by Detroit (serious mistake), Daly signed with the struggling Nets. But there was hope in the Meadowlands, with Drazen Petrovic, Derrick Coleman,

and Kenny Anderson. Daly was just the right type of hired hand to whip the troops into shape.

Under previous administrations, the Nets were a franchise in turmoil. The players didn't talk to the coach; some players didn't talk to their teammates; even the owners were barely on speaking terms. If ever there was a team crying out for leadership, it was New Jersey.

Beginning from day one, the two old gunfighters slugged it out on the not-so-dusty pavement of the New York metropolitan area. Riley had the Knicks playing an aggressive (some said too aggressive) style of defense and adding a little outside shooting to go with their power game inside. Daly rescued Anderson from the depths of the Nets' bench, got Coleman and Chris Morris to provide sparks inside, and let Petrovic light up the scoreboard with "treys." (Drazen Petrovic was killed in a tragic automobile accident soon after the 1993 regular season.)

Though the first round went to the Knicks, the Atlantic Division champs in '93, the Nets are loaded for bear and ready to charge to the top in '94.

★ WHAT NEXT? A FOUR-PEAT??? ★

THE INCREDI-BULLS AGAIN!

Whoever dreamed that the major pre-season activity for 1994 would be inventing a new way to spell four-in-a-row? Certainly not the fans in New York and Phoenix, each of whom was certain that the reigning champion Chicago Bulls would fall before their mighty Knicks or Suns, respectively. Yet when the Arizona desert dust cleared last summer (and it *was* summer), there were the Bulls with their hard-fought three-peat victory and the best chance in decades for four-on-the-floor.

Can the Bulls four-peat? Are they the quad-squad? Can they win a double-double? Without Michael, probably not.

The key ingredient is gone. As long as no. 23 was doing his thing, you could never count the Bulls out. Michael proved that in the Phoenix finale when he scored every one of Chicago's fourth-quarter points prior to Jim Paxon's game-winning hoop. You could see it in Michael's eyes: Give me the ball, it's my game. And so it was. During the Phoenix series, Jordan averaged 41 points per game, an all-time record. And the Bulls needed just about every one of them.

Jordan won his third straight Finals MVP Award, something no other human has ever accomplished. And while rumors swirled around that Michael wasn't focused on basketball, that he was having money problems, he simply went out and proved again that he is the best player on earth.

The rest of the Bulls contributed, of course. Scottie Pippin, of Dream Team fame, was the hero of the New York series for the Eastern Conference championship. The Knicks, with the superior regular-season record, owned the home-court advantage. And when they won the first two games at home, it looked like the Bulls were dead. Enter Pippin (and Horace Grant, playing the best basketball of his career), and the Knicks fell in six, including a memorable Bulls game-five win at Madison Square Garden where the Knicks "never lost." Of course, it didn't hurt that Michael threw in 54 points in game four and 29 and 25, respectively, in the final two outings.

And now comes that four-peat. Some basketball experts see the Bulls '92–93 title pretenders, the Knicks and Suns, meeting for the '94 crown.

And without Michael, they might have the four-sight needed to win a championship.

In retiring, Michael Jeffrey Jordan proudly pointed to his three rings (perfect for the media circus that is the NBA) and insisted he had no more worlds to conquer. It was a lot easier for Larry Bird and Magic Johnson to stay focused; they were constantly battling each other for the NBA crown. Michael had no such similar rival, with the possible exception of Phoenix's loose cannon, Charles Barkley. And Michael only outscored him by 14 points per game when they met last June!

Meanwhile, Chicago general manager Jerry Krause hasn't stood still. While he searches for replacement parts for his lumbering front court (Bill Cartwright, Scott Williams, and Will Perdue) and a shooting guard to take over from Finals hero Paxson, Toni Kukoc is on his way. The 6–10 Yugoslav, perhaps Europe's finest player, should make the Bulls that much stronger in '94. For the future, Krause drafted wide-body 6–9 Corie Blount from Cincinnati, a major shot-blocker who should be ready soon.

BILL RUSSELL
BOSTON CELTICS

★

WILT CHAMBERLAIN
PHILADELPHIA WARRIORS

★ WHEN TITANS CLASHED ★

t was the classic war. The combatants didn't like each other. Their teams didn't like each other. Their fans downright hated the opposing fans. It matched the two premier big men in basketball. In a game where many men their size had been clumsy clods, they were athletes. One was the master of offense, the other the master of defense. It didn't get any better than this.

Whenever and wherever Bill Russell of the Boston Celtics and Wilt Chamberlain of the Philadelphia Warriors got together, sparks were sure to fly. They packed the house at the Boston Garden, or Philadelphia Convention Hall, or Madison Square Garden. A Chamberlain-Russell (or a Russell-Chamberlain) clash always found the press tables full.

In almost every respect, the two men were opposites. Russell stood for defense. He changed the way defense was played in the NBA. With a shot-blocker and rebounder like Russell playing close to the bucket, his Celtics were able to play defense more aggressively on the outside. They knew the big guy would clean up whatever mess they made.

Russel won the NBA Most Valuable Player award five times during his stellar career. Four times he was the league rebounding champion. Yet he never averaged as many as 20 points per game in any season.

Chamberlain, on the other hand, was unstoppable on offense. During one season (1962), he *averaged* 50.4 ppg, including one unforgettable 100-point outburst against the New York Knicks at Hershey, Pennsylvania. At one point, he led the league in scoring seven straight times, a record tied in '93 by Michael Jordan.

Russell was a practical unknown in high school (McClymonds in Oakland, California). He didn't really play until his senior year and didn't have much choice about playing college ball. He went to the University of San Francisco and promptly led the Dons to two straight national championships. Then he paced the United States team to the gold medal at the 1956 Olympics in Melbourne, Australia.

Coach Red Auerbach of the Celtics was so excited about the prospect of having Russell lead his team that he traded two All-Pros (Cliff Hagen and Ed Macauley) to the St. Louis Hawks for the right to pick Bill as the third-choice in the NBA draft.

Chaimberlain, on the other hand, was famous by the time he got to Overbrook High School in Philadelphia. He also played against college and pro stars during the summers at upstate New York resorts. In those days, NBA teams were allowed to select—before the draft—college players who played near their cities. The Philadelphia Warriors knew that Wilt would be going to the University of Kansas, so they asked for and were granted permission to take the Big Dipper as a territorial choice right out of high school.

At Kansas, Wilt was confronted by every kind of defense opposing coaches could think of. In fact, NCAA rules were altered to limit his domination. Yet, unlike Russell, Wilt never led KU to a college championship. His Jayhawks lost a triple-overtime thriller to North Carolina for the 1957 title. Wilt then played one year for the Harlem Globtrotters before joining the Warriors when his college class graduated.

When Chamberlain came along, Russell was ready. He had made the blocked shot into an art form. Opposing players knew they'd have to beat Russ before they could get a lay-up. On the other hand, Philadelphia won Wilt's first three pro games (Wilt had 36 points and 34 rebounds in one of them) before the first-ever matchup with Russell on November 7, 1959.

Boston Garden was a complete sellout. It had been for weeks. Tickets were being scalped on the streets for a week's salary. At 7–1, Wilt was bigger (by four inches) and heavier (by 30 pounds) than his Boston rival. He was, perhaps, the better ball-handler and, definitely, the better shooter. But nobody played defense like Russell.

In that first game, Bill got in Wilt's face early. He blocked a couple of fall-away jumpers (no one had ever done *that* before!) and Wilt was shut down. Boston won easily, 115–106.

Through the years, they met more than 140 times. Russ scored 14.5 and had 23.7 rebounds on average. Chamberlain scored 28.7 points and grabbed 28.7 rebounds per game. But Russell's Celtics won about 60% of the time—which is, after all, what it's all about.

★ THE MEGASTARS: BY THE NUMBERS ★

★

CHARLES BARKLEY, Forward
Height: 6–6   Weight: 252 lbs.   Born: February 20, 1963
College: Auburn
Birthplace: Leeds, AL
Professional Career: 1984–1992, Philadelphia 76ers;
1992–93, Phoenix Suns

★

PATRICK EWING, Center
Height: 7–0   Weight: 240 lbs.   Born: February 20, 1963
College: Georgetown
Birthplace: Kingston, Jamaica
Professional Career: 1985–93, New York Knicks

★

KEVIN JOHNSON, Guard
Height: 6–1   Weight: 190 lbs.   Born: March 4, 1966
College: California (Berkeley)
Birthplace: Sacramento, CA
Professional Career: 1987–88, Cleveland Cavaliers;
1988–93, Phoenix Suns

★

LARRY JOHNSON, Forward
Height: 6–7   Weight: 250 lbs.   Born: March 14, 1969
College: Nevada-Las Vegas
Birthplace: Dallas, TX
Professional Career: 1991–93, Charlotte Hornets

★

MICHAEL JORDAN, Guard
Height: 6–6   Weight: 198 lbs.   Born: February 17, 1963
College: North Carolina
Birthplace: Brooklyn, NY
Professional Career: 1984–93, Chicago Bulls

★

KARL MALONE, Forward
Height: 6–9   Weight: 256 lbs.   Born: July 24, 1963
College: Louisiana Tech
Birthplace: Summerfield, LA
Professional Career: 1985–93, Utah Jazz

★

ALONZO MOURNING, Center
Height: 6–10   Weight: 240 lbs.   Born: February 8, 1970
College: Georgetown
Birthplace: Chesapeake, VA
Professional Career: 1992–93, Charlotte Hornets

★

SHAQUILLE O'NEAL, Center
Height: 7–1   Weight: 303 lbs.   Born: March 6, 1972
College: Louisiana State
Birthplace: Newark, NJ
Professional Career: 1992–93, Orlando Magic

★

MARK PRICE, Guard
Height: 6–0   Weight: 178 lbs.   Born: February 15, 1964
College: Georgia Tech
Birthplace: Bartlesville, OK
Professional Career: 1986–93, Cleveland Cavaliers

★

DAVID ROBINSON, Center
Height: 7–0   Weight: 235 lbs.   Born: August 6, 1965
College: U. S. Naval Academy
Birthplace: Key West, FL
Professional Career: 1989–93, San Antonio Spurs

★

JOHN STOCKTON, Guard
Height: 6–1   Weight: 175 lbs.   Born: March 26, 1962
College: Gonzaga Univ.
Birthplace: Spokane, WA
Professional Career: 1984–93, Utah Jazz

★

DOMINIQUE WILKINS, Forward
Height: 6–8   Weight: 218 lbs.   Born: January 12, 1960
College: Univ. of Georgia
Birthplace: Sorbonne, France
Professional Career: 1983–93, Atlanta Hawks